Vegetarian Air Fryer Cookbook

Affordable, Quick & Healthy Vegetarian Air Fryer Recipes For beginners and Advanced Users

Alissa Peterson

Disclaimer Notice:

Please note the information contained within this document is for educational and entertainment purposes only. All effort has been executed to present accurate, up to date, and reliable, complete information. No warranties of any kind are declared or implied. Readers acknowledge that the author is not engaging in the rendering of legal, financial, medical or professional advice. The content within this book has been derived from various sources. Please consult a licensed professional before attempting any techniques outlined in this book.

By reading this document, the reader agrees that under no circumstances is the author responsible for any losses, direct or indirect, which are incurred as a result of the use of information contained within this document, including, but not limited to, errors, omissions, or inaccuracies.

Table of Content

Introduction

Congratulations on purchasing your copy of **Vegetarian Air Fryer Cookbook: Affordable, Quick & Healthy Vegetarian Air Fryer Recipes For beginners and Advanced Users**, and thank you for doing so.

I'm glad you chose to take this opportunity to welcome the air fryer diet into your life. I'm sure this book will help you find all the information and tools you need to better integrate the Air Fryer Diet plan with your habits.

In addition, I thought I'd share with you some delicious ideas and recipes for all tastes and the best of your low carb diet that I hope you'll enjoy.

You'll find hundreds of easy-to-make ideas that will best suit your situation or needs of the moment, with all the preparation times, portion sizes and a list of all the nutritional values you'll need.

RECIPES

Grille Tomatoes with Garden Herb Salad

Servings: 4

Cooking Time: 20 minutes

INGREDIENTS

- 3 large green tomatoes 1 clove of garlic, minced 5 tablespoons olive oil Salt and pepper to taste

- ¾ cup fresh parsley, chopped

- ¾ cup cilantro leaves, chopped

- ½ cup chopped chives 4 leaves iceberg lettuce

- ¼ cup hazelnuts, toasted and chopped

- ¼ cup pistachios, toasted and chopped

- ¼ cup golden raisins

- 2 tablespoons white balsamic vinegar

DIRECTIONS

1   Preheat the air fryer at 3500F.

2   Place the grill pan accessory in the air fryer.

3   In a mixing bowl, season the tomatoes with garlic, oil, salt and pepper to taste.

4   Place on the grill pan and grill for 20 minutes.

5   Once the tomatoes are done, toss in a salad bowl together with the rest of the ingredients.

NUTRITION: Calories: 287; Carbs: 12.2g; Protein: 4.8g; Fat: 25.9g

Shrimp and Radish Mix

Preparation time: 5 minutes Cooking time: 20 minutes

Servings: 4

INGREDIENTS

•	1 pound shrimp, peeled, deveined and minced

•	1 cup radishes, halved

•	½ cup spring onions, chopped 1 tablespoon olive oil

•	1 tablespoon lemon juice

•	1 tablespoon parsley, chopped Salt and black pepper to

the taste

DIRECTIONS

1.	In the air fryer's pan, mix the shrimp with the radishes

and the other ingredients, put the pan in the machine and

cook at 360 degrees F for 14 minutes.

2.	Divide into bowls and serve as an appetizer.

NUTRITION: Calories 271, Fat 15, Fiber 3, Carbs

4, Protein 14

Tasty Tofu

Cooking Time: 12 minutes Servings: 4

INGREDIENTS

- ¼ cup cornmeal

- 15-ounces extra firm tofu, drained, cubed Salt and

pepper to taste

- 1 teaspoon chili flakes

- ¾ cup cornstarch

DIRECTIONS

1. Line the air fryer basket with aluminum foil and brush

with oil.

2. Preheat your air fryer to 370°Fahrenheit.

3. Mix all ingredients in a bowl. Place in air fryer and cook

for 12-minutes.

NUTRITION: Calories: 246, Total Fat: 11.2g, Carbs: 8.7g,

Protein: 7.6g

Bacon Dip

Preparation time: 5 minutes Cooking time: 20 minutes

Servings: 8

INGREDIENTS

- 2 tablespoons butter, melted 1 cup cream cheese, soft

- 1 cup bacon, chopped

- ½ teaspoon sweet paprika

- 3 cups spring onions, chopped A pinch of salt and black

pepper 1 tablespoon chives, chopped

DIRECTIONS

1. In the air fryer's pan, mix the melted butter with the

bacon and the other ingredients, introduce the pan in the

machine and cook at and 380 degrees F for 20 minutes.

2. Divide into bowls and serve as a party dip.

NUTRITION: Calories 220, Fat 12, Fiber 2, Carbs

4, Protein 15

Spanish Potatoes

Preparation time: 10 minutes

Cooking time: 57 minutes Servings: 2

INGREDIENTS

- 400 g potato

- Water

- 1 tbsp olive oil

- Salt

DIRECTIONS

1. Peel and cut the potato in julienne about

2. 0.5 CM thick.

3. Prepare a bowl with very cold water, if necessary, add ice. Place the cut potatoes for at least 30 minutes to make them starch.

4. Dry each potato with an absorbent napkin and place in another dry bowl.

5. When they are all dry, sprinkle with oil or brush with olive oil and season with salt and whatever you like (sweet paprika, oregano, etc.).

6.   In this case place in a fryer without oil at temperature 1600C for 17 minutes.

7.   Set the fryer at 1800C another 10 minutes and that's it.

NUTRITION: Calories 77 Fat 0.09g Carbohydrate17.47g Sugars 0.78g Protein2.02g Cholesterol 0mg

Crispy Kale Chips

Cooking Time: 3 minutes Servings: 2

INGREDIENTS

- 1 head of kale

- 1 teaspoon soy sauce 1 tablespoon olive oil

DIRECTIONS

1. Tear up kale into 1 ½-inch pieces. Wash clean and dry thoroughly.

2. Toss with olive oil and soy sauce. Fry in air fryer at 390° Fahrenheit for 3-minutes.

NUTRITION: Calories: 243, Total Fat: 7.6g, Carbs: 6.4g, Protein: 14.3g

Roasted Corn

Cooking Time: 10 minutes Servings: 8

INGREDIENTS

- 4 ears of corn

- Salt and pepper to taste 3 teaspoons vegetable oil

DIRECTIONS

1. Remove the husks from corn, wash and pat them dry. Cut if needed to fit into air fryer basket.

2. Drizzle with vegetable oil and season with salt and pepper.

3. Cook at 400°Fahrenheit for 10-minutes. NUTRITION: Calories: 256, Total Fat: 9.4g, Carbs: 8.7g, Protein: 9.2g

Garlic Mushrooms

Preparation time: 10 minutes

Cooking time: 10 minutes Servings: 2

INGREDIENTS

- 1 slice of white bread

- 1 crushed garlic clove

- 1 tbsp chopped parsley

- Freshly ground black pepper

- 1 tbsp olive oil

- 12 mushrooms

DIRECTIONS

1. Preheat the air fryer to 200°C.

2. Grate the slice of bread until it is thin in the kitchen robot and mix it with the garlic, parsley, and season to taste. Finally, pour the olive oil.

3. Remove the mushroom stems and fill the caps with the breadcrumbs.

4. Place the mushrooms in the basket and place it in the air fryer. Set the timer to 10 minutes. Bake until golden brown and crispy.

5.   Serve them on a tray.

NUTRITION: Calories 139 Fat 11.6g Carbohydrates 6.1g

Sugars 3.5gprotein 4.7g Cholesterol 30.4mg

Roasted Potatoes with Paprika and Greek Yogurt

Preparation time: 10 minutes

Cooking time: 20 minutes Servings: 4

INGREDIENTS

- 800 g of white potatoes

- 2 tbsp olive oil

- 1 tbsp spicy paprika

- Freshly ground black pepper

- 150 ml Greek yogurt

DIRECTIONS

1. Preheat the air fryer to 180oC. Peel the potatoes and cut them into cubes of 3 cm. Dip the cubes in water for at least 30 minutes. Dry them well with paper towels.

2. In a medium-sized bowl, mix 1 tablespoon of olive oil with the paprika and add pepper to taste. Coat the potato dice with the spiced oil.

3. Place the potato dice in the fryer basket and place it in the air fryer. Set the timer to 20 minutes and fry the dice until golden brown and ready to take. Spin them occasionally.

4.   In a small bowl, mix the Greek yogurt with the remaining tablespoon of olive oil and add salt and pepper to taste. Spread the paprika over the mixture. Serve the yogurt as a sauce with the potatoes.

5.   Serve the potato dice on a tray and salt them. They will be delicious with ribs or kebabs.

NUTRITION: Calories 225.1 Fat 13.8 G Carbohydrate 24.2 G Sugars 9.7 G Protein2.5 G Cholesterol 0.0 Mg

Grilled Green Beans with Shallots

Servings: 6

Cooking Time: 25 minutes

INGREDIENTS

•   1-pound fresh green beans, trimmed 2 large shallots, sliced

•   1 tablespoon vegetable oil 1 teaspoon soy sauce

•   2 tablespoons fresh basil, chopped

•   1 tablespoon fresh mint, chopped

•   1 tablespoon sesame seeds, toasted 2 tablespoons pine nuts

DIRECTIONS

1   Preheat the air fryer at 350oF.

2   Place the grill pan accessory in the air fryer. In a mixing bowl, combine the green beans,

3   shallots, vegetable oil, and soy sauce.

4   Dump in the air fryer and cook for 25 minutes.

5   Once cooked, garnish with basil, mints, sesame seeds, and pine nuts.

NUTRITION: Calories:307; Carbs: 11.2g; Protein: 23.7g; Fat: 19.7g

Grilled Sweet Potato Wedges with Dipping Sauce

Servings: 3

Cooking Time: 20 minutes

INGREDIENTS

- 3 medium sweet potatoes, peeled and sliced 2 tablespoons olive oil

- Salt and pepper to taste

- ½ cup sour cream

- ½ cup mayonnaise

- 2 tablespoons fresh chives, chopped 3 tablespoons Asiago cheese, grated 2 tablespoons parmesan cheese

DIRECTIONS

1   Preheat the air fryer at 3500F.

2   Place the grill pan accessory in the air fryer.

3   Brush the potatoes with olive oil and drizzle with salt and pepper to taste.

4   Place on the grill pan and cook for 20 minutes.

5   Meanwhile, mix the sour cream, mayonnaise, fresh chives, Asiago cheese, and parmesan cheese in a bowl.

6   Season with salt and pepper to taste.

7   Serve the potatoes with the sauce.

NUTRITION: Calories: 625; Carbs: 50.5g; Protein: 12.7g; Fat: 42.3g

Orange Mango Salad

Preparation time: 5 minutes Cooking time: 8 minutes

Servings: 4

INGREDIENTS

- 1 cup mango, peeled and cubed 1 cup baby spinach

- 1 cup cherry tomatoes, halved

- 1 cup oranges, peeled and cut into segments 1 tablespoon olive oil

- 1 tablespoon balsamic vinegar 2 teaspoons orange zest, grated A handful parsley, chopped

DIRECTIONS

1. In the air fryer's pan, mix the mango with the spinach and the other ingredients, toss and cook at 350 degrees F for 8 minutes.

2. Divide into bowls and serve. NUTRITION: Calories 151, Fat 6, Fiber 6, Carbs

11, Protein 5

Crispy Herb Cauliflower Florets

Cooking Time: 20 minutes Servings: 2

INGREDIENTS

- 2 egg, beaten

- 2 tablespoons parmesan cheese, grated 2 cups cauliflower florets, boiled

- ¼ cup almond flour

- 1 tablespoon olive oil Salt to taste

- ½ tablespoon mixed herbs

- ½ teaspoon chili powder

- ½ teaspoon garlic powder

- ½ cup breadcrumbs

DIRECTIONS

1. In a bowl, combine garlic powder, breadcrumbs, chili powder, mixed herbs, salt, and cheese.

2. Add olive oil to the breadcrumb mixture and mix well.

3. Place flour in a bowl and place the egg in another bowl.

4. Dip the cauliflower florets into the beaten egg, then in flour, and coat with breadcrumbs.

5. Preheat your air fryer to 350° Fahrenheit.

6.   Place the coated cauliflower florets inside air fryer basket and cook for 20-minutes.

NUTRITION: Calories: 253, Total Fat: 11.3g, Carbs: 9,5g, Protein: 8.5g

Spicy Nuts

Cooking Time: 4 minutes Servings: 8

INGREDIENTS

- 2 cups mixed nuts

- 1 teaspoon chipotle chili powder 1 teaspoon salt

- 1 teaspoon pepper

- 1 tablespoon butter, melted 1 teaspoon ground cumin

DIRECTIONS

1. In a bowl, add all ingredients and toss to coat.

2. Preheat your air fryer to 350°Fahrenheit for

3. 5-minutes.

4. Add mixed nuts into air fryer basket and roast for 4-minutes.

NUTRITION: Calories: 252, Total Fat: 8.6g, Carbs: 7.2g, Protein: 8.4g

Crispy Cheese Sticks

Cooking Time: 5 minutes Servings: 4

INGREDIENTS

• 1 (16-ounce) package mozzarella cheese

• ½ teaspoon salt

• 1 teaspoon garlic powder 1 teaspoon onion powder

• 1 teaspoon cayenne pepper 1 cup breadcrumbs

• 1 cup almond flour 2 eggs, beaten

DIRECTIONS

1. Cut the mozzarella cheese into 3 (1/2 inch) sticks.

2. Add beaten eggs in small bowl. In a bowl, add flour.

3. In another small bowl, combine breadcrumbs, cayenne pepper, onion powder, garlic powder, and salt.

4. Dip cheese sticks into beaten egg, then dip into flour, then return to egg, and coat with breadcrumbs.

5. Place coated cheese in the fridge for 20- minutes. Preheat your air fryer to 400° Fahrenheit.

6. Spray air fryer basket with cooking spray.

7. Place the coated cheese sticks into air fryer and cook for 5-minutes.

8. Serve hot!

NUTRITION: Calories: 242, Total Fat: 11.2g, Carbs: 9.4g,

Protein: 9.7g

Air-Fried Crispy Zucchini

Cooking Time: 20 minutes Servings: 6

INGREDIENTS

- 4 egg whites

- 6 medium zucchinis, thinly sliced

- 4 tablespoons parmesan cheese, grated

- ½ teaspoon garlic powder 1 cup breadcrumbs

- Salt and pepper to taste

DIRECTIONS

1. Preheat your air fryer to 400° Fahrenheit.

2. Whisk salt, pepper and egg whites in small bowl. In another bowl, combine garlic powder, breadcrumbs, and parmesan cheese.

3. Dip zucchini slices into egg whites then coat them with breadcrumbs.

4. Place coated zucchini in air fryer basket and cook for 20-minutes.

NUTRITION: Calories: 247, Total Fat: 9.4g, Carbs: 8.6g, Protein: 9.2g

Green Salad with Roasted Pepper

Preparation time: 15 minutes

Cooking time: 10 minutes Servings: 4

INGREDIENTS

- 1 red pepper

- 1 tbsp lemon juice

- 3 tbsp yogurt

- 2 tbsp olive oil

- Freshly ground black pepper

- 1 romaine lettuce in wide strips

- 50 g arugula leaves

DIRECTIONS

1.	Preheat the air fryer to 200°C.

2.	Place the pepper in the basket and place it in the air fryer. Set the timer to 10 minutes and roast the pepper until the skin is slightly burned.

3.	Place the pepper in a bowl and cover it with a lid or with transparent film. Let stand 10 to 15 minutes.

4.	Next, cut the pepper into four parts and remove the seeds and skin. Cut the pepper into strips.

5.   Mix a dressing in a bowl with 2 tablespoons of the pepper juice, lemon juice, yogurt, and olive oil. Add pepper and salt to taste.

6.   Pour the lettuce and arugula leaves into the dressing and garnish the salad with the pepper strips.

NUTRITION: Calories 77.9 Fat 0.4 G Carbohydrate 19.3 G Sugars4.6 G Protein2.7 G Cholesterol 0.0 Mg

Avocado and Green Beans Bowls

Preparation time: 5 minutes Cooking time: 12 minutes

Servings: 4

INGREDIENTS

- 2 avocados, peeled, pitted and cut into wedges

- ½ pound green beans, trimmed and halved 1 cup kalamata olives, pitted and halved

- 1 cup cherry tomatoes, halved 1 tablespoon olive oil

- A pinch of salt and black pepper

DIRECTIONS

1. In the air fryer's pan, mix the avocados with the green beans and the other ingredients, toss, put the pan in the

2. machine and cook at 370 degrees F for 12 minutes.

3. Divide into bowls and serve as an appetizer.

NUTRITION: Calories 200, Fat 12, Fiber 3, Carbs 5, Protein 16

Potato Tots

Cooking Time: 8 minutes Servings: 2

INGREDIENTS

- 1 large potato, diced Salt and pepper to taste

- 1 teaspoon onion, minced 1 tablespoon olive oil

DIRECTIONS

1. Cover potatoes with water in saucepan and boil over medium-high heat.

2. Drain the potatoes and place in a bowl and mash potatoes.

3. Add olive oil, onion, pepper and salt to mashed potatoes and mix well.

4. Make small tots from potato mixture and place into air fryer basket.

5. Cook at 380°Fahrenheit for 8-minutes. Shake basket and cook for another 5- minutes.

6. Serve hot!

NUTRITION: Calories: 252, Total Fat: 8.7g, Carbs: 7.8g, Protein: 8.2g

Avocado Salad

Preparation time: 5 minutes Cooking time: 5 minutes

Servings: 4

INGREDIENTS

- red onion, sliced

- cups avocado, peeled, pitted and cubed 1 cup cherry tomatoes, halved

- 2 tablespoons avocado oil Juice of 1 lime

- Salt and black pepper to the taste 1 cup walnuts, chopped

- 1 tablespoon chives, chopped

DIRECTIONS

In your air fryer, mix the avocado with the tomatoes and the other ingredients, toss, cook at 400 degrees F for 5 minutes, divide into bowls and serve.

NUTRITION: Calories 151, Fat 4, Fiber 6,

Carbs 9,

Protein 4

Tuna and Shrimp Mix

Preparation time: 5 minutes Cooking time: 10 minutes

Servings: 2

INGREDIENTS

- 1 pound tuna, skinless, boneless and cubed
- ½ pound shrimp, peeled and deveined 1 cup cherry tomatoes, halved
- 1 cup baby spinach
- 1 chili pepper, minced 2 tablespoon olive oil
- 1 tablespoon lemon juice
- A pinch of salt and black pepper

DIRECTIONS

1. In a pan that fits your air fryer, mix all the ingredients, toss, introduce in the fryer and cook at 360 degrees F for 10 minutes.

2. Divide into bowls and serve as an appetizer.

NUTRITION: Calories 231, Fat 18, Fiber 3, Carbs 4, Protein 18

Spicy Tomatoes

Preparation time: 5 minutes Cooking time: 15 minutes

Servings: 4

INGREDIENTS

•   1 pound cherry tomatoes, halved 1 teaspoon chili powder

•   1 teaspoon hot paprika

•   1 jalapenos, chopped Juice of 1 lime

•   2 tablespoon olive oil 2 garlic cloves, minced

•   Salt and black pepper to the taste

DIRECTIONS

1.   In the air fryer's pan, combine the tomatoes with the chili powder and the other ingredients, toss and cook at 350 degrees F for 15 minutes.

2.   Divide between plates and serve. NUTRITION: Calories 174, Fat 5, Fiber 7, Carbs 11, Protein 4

Indian Grilled Vegetables

Servings: 6

Cooking Time: 20 minutes

INGREDIENTS

- ½ cup yogurt

- cloves of garlic, minced

- 2-inch fresh ginger, minced

- 3 tablespoons Tandoori spice blend

- 2 tablespoons canola oil

- 2 small onions, cut into wedges

- 1 small zucchini, cut into thick slices

- 1 carrot, peeled and shaved to 1/8-inch thick 1 yellow

sweet pepper, seeded and chopped

- ½ head cauliflower, cut into florets 1 handful sugar

snap peas

- 1 cup young ears of corn

DIRECTIONS

1   Preheat the air fryer at 3500F.

2   Place the grill pan accessory in the air fryer.

3   In a Ziploc bag, put all ingredients and give a shake to season all vegetables.

4   Dump all ingredients on the grill pan and cook for 20 minutes.

5   Make sure to give the vegetables a shake halfway through the cooking time.

NUTRITION: Calories:126; Carbs: 17.9g; Protein: 2.9g; Fat: 6.1g

Tomato and Shrimp Salad

Preparation time: 6 minutes Cooking time: 6

minutes Servings: 4

INGREDIENTS

- 1 pound cherry tomatoes, halved

- ½ pound shrimp, peeled and deveined Juice of 1 lime

- 1 cup baby kale

- 2 green onions, chopped 2 tomatoes, cubed

- jalapeno pepper, chopped 1 tablespoon olive oil

- teaspoons chili powder

- Salt and black pepper to the taste

DIRECTIONS

1. In a pan that fits your air fryer, mix the tomatoes with the shrimp, oil and the other ingredients, toss, introduce the pan in the fryer and cook at 400 degrees F for 6 minutes.

2. Divide the mix into bowls and serve. NUTRITION: Calories 200, Fat 4, Fiber 7, Carbs

12, Protein 6

Spicy Green Beans Mix

Preparation time: 5 minutes Cooking time: 15 minutes

Servings: 4

INGREDIENTS

- 1 pound green beans, trimmed and halved 2 red chilies, minced

- 1 tablespoon lemon juice 1 tablespoon olive oil

- 1 teaspoon hot paprika

- A pinch of salt and black pepper

- tablespoons chives, chopped

DIRECTIONS

1. In a pan that fits your air fryer, mix the green beans with the chilies and the other ingredients, toss, introduce in the fryer and cook at 320 degrees F for 15 minutes.

2. Divide between plates and serve right away.

NUTRITION: Calories 124, Fat 6, Fiber 6, Carbs 16, Protein 7

Roast Celeriac

Preparation time: 10 minutes Cooking time: 15 minutes

Servings: 4

INGREDIENTS

- 2 cups celeriac, peeled and roughly cubed 2 tablespoons olive oil

- Juice of 1 lime

- A pinch of salt and black pepper

- ½ tablespoon chives, chopped

DIRECTIONS

1. In the air fryer, combine the celeriac with the oil and the other ingredients, toss and cook at 380 degrees F for 15 minutes.

2. Divide between plates and serve. NUTRITION: Calories 124, Fat 1, Fiber 4, Carbs 6, Protein 6

Maple Corn

Preparation time: 5 minutes Cooking time: 15 minutes

Servings: 4

INGREDIENTS

- 2 cups corn

- 1 tablespoon avocado oil Juice of 1 lime

- 1 tablespoon maple syrup

- Salt and black pepper to the taste

- 1 tablespoon chives, chopped

DIRECTIONS

1. In the air fryer, combine the corn with the oil and the other ingredients, toss and cook at 390 degrees F for 15 minutes.

2. Divide the mix between plates and serve. NUTRITION: Calories 100, Fat 2, Fiber 3, Carbs 8,

Protein 3

Grilled Vegetables with Garlic

Servings: 4

Cooking Time: 15 minutes

INGREDIENTS

- 1 package frozen chopped vegetables 1 red onion, sliced

- 1 cup baby Portobello mushrooms, chopped Salt and

pepper to taste

- 4 cloves of garlic, minced

- 3 tablespoon red wine vinegar

- ¼ cup chopped fresh basil

- 1 ½ tablespoons honey1 teaspoon Dijon mustard

- 1/3 cup olive oil

DIRECTIONS

1   Preheat the air fryer at 350oF.

2   Place the grill pan accessory in the air fryer.

3   In a Ziploc bag, combine the vegetables and season with

salt, pepper, and garlic.

4   Give a good shake to combine everything.

5   Dump on to the grill pan and cook for 15 minutes.

6   Meanwhile, combine the rest of the Ingredients in a bowl and season with more salt and pepper.

7   Drizzle the grilled vegetables with the sauce.

8   Serve and enjoy. NUTRITION: Calories: 200; Carbs: 8.3g; Protein: 2.1g; Fat: 18.2g

Green Beans and Avocado Mix

Preparation time: 10 minutes Cooking time: 20 minutes

Servings: 4

INGREDIENTS

• 2 pounds green beans, trimmed and halved 1 cup avocado, peeled, pitted and cubed

• 1 cup mango, peeled and cubed 1 tablespoon olive oil

• 1 teaspoon chili powder

• 1 tablespoon lemon zest, grated 1 tablespoon lemon juice

• Salt and black pepper to the taste

DIRECTIONS

1. In the air fryer's pan, combine the green beans with the avocado and the other ingredients, toss and cook at 360 degrees F for 20 minutes.

2. Divide between plates and serve. NUTRITION: Calories 108, Fat 4, Fiber 8, Carbs 17.4, Protein 4.4

Curry Green Beans

Preparation time: 5 minutes Cooking time: 20 minutes

Servings: 4

INGREDIENTS

• 1 pound green beans, trimmed and halved 1 tablespoon green curry paste

• 1 tablespoons butter, melted 1 teaspoon curry powder

• ¼ cup veggie stock

• 1 teaspoon sweet paprika

• A pinch of salt and black pepper 1 tablespoon chives, chopped

DIRECTIONS

1. In your air fryer's pan, mix the green beans with the curry paste and the other ingredients, toss and cook at 360 degrees F for 20 minutes.

2. Divide everything between plates and serve.

NUTRITION: Calories 194, Fat 4, Fiber 4, Carbs 8.4, Protein 7

Grilled Asparagus with Hollandaise Sauce

Servings: 6

Cooking Time: 15 minutes

INGREDIENTS

Servings: 6

Cooking Time: 15 minutes

INGREDIENTS

- 3 pounds asparagus spears, trimmed 2 tablespoons

olive oil

- ½ teaspoon salt

- ¼ teaspoon black pepper 3 egg yolks

- ½ lemon juice

- ½ teaspoon salt

- A pinch of mustard powder

- A punch of ground white pepper

- ½ cup butter, melted

- 1 teaspoon chopped tarragon leaves

DIRECTIONS

1   Preheat the air fryer at 3500F.

2   Place the grill pan accessory in the air fryer.

3   In a Ziploc bag, combine the asparagus, olive oil, salt and pepper. Give a good shake to combine everything.

4   Dump on to the grill pan and cook for 15 minutes.

5   Meanwhile, on a double boiler over medium flame, whisk the egg yolks, lemon juice, and salt until silky. Add in the mustard powder, white pepper and melted butter.

6   Keep whisking until the sauce is smooth. Garnish with tarragon leaves.

7   Drizzle the sauce over asparagus spears.

NUTRITION: Calories: 253; Carbs: 10.2g; Protein: 6.7g; Fat: 22.4g

Zucchini and Avocado Mix

Preparation time: 5 minutes Cooking time: 15 minutes

Servings: 4

INGREDIENTS

- 1 pound zucchinis, roughly cubed

- 1 cup avocado, peeled, pitted and cubed 1 tablespoon

olive oil

- Juice of 1 lime

- 1 teaspoon nutmeg, ground

- Salt and black pepper to the taste

- ½ teaspoon garlic powder

- 1 tablespoon chives, chopped

DIRECTIONS

1. In the air fryer's pan, mix the zucchinis with the

avocado and the other ingredients, toss and cook at 360

degrees F for 15 minutes.

2. Divide between plates and serve. NUTRITION: Calories

210, Fat 5, Fiber 7, Carbs 12, Protein 5

Bell Peppers Salad

Preparation time: 10 minutes Cooking time: 15 minutes

Servings: 4

INGREDIENTS

- 2 red bell peppers, cut into strips

- 2 green bell peppers, cut into strips 2 orange bell peppers, cut into strips 1 cup cherry tomatoes, halved

- cup baby spinach Juice of 1 lime

- tablespoons olive oil

- Salt and black pepper to the taste

DIRECTIONS

1. In a pan that fits your air fryer, mix the peppers with the tomatoes and the other ingredients, toss, introduce the pan in the fryer and cook at 360 degrees F for 15 minutes.

2. Divide into bowls and serve. NUTRITION: Calories 161, Fat 7, Fiber 6, Carbs

12, Protein 7

Roasted Air Fried Vegetables

Servings: 4

Cooking Time: 15 minutes

INGREDIENTS

• 12 small red potatoes, scrubbed and halved 1 cup chopped carrots

• 1 cup butternut squash, peeled and chopped 1 cup red onion, diced

• 1 red pepper, chopped 1 tablespoon olive oil 1 teaspoon thyme

• 1 teaspoon basil

• 1 teaspoon Italian seasoning

• ½ teaspoon garlic powder Salt and pepper to taste

DIRECTIONS

1. Preheat the air fryer at 375OF.

2. Place the grill pan accessory in the air fryer.

3. In a mixing bowl, toss all Ingredients until well-combined.

4. Place on the grill pan and cook for 15 minutes.

5.   Stir the vegetables halfway through the cooking time to grill evenly.

NUTRITION: Calories: 127; Carbs: 22.4g; Protein: 2.6g

Dill Mango and Corn

Preparation time: 5 minutes Cooking time: 12 minutes

Servings: 4

INGREDIENTS

- 2 cups corn

- 1 cup mango, peeled and cubed

- 1 cup baby spinach

- 1 tablespoon olive oil Juice of 1 lime

- Salt and black pepper to the taste

- 2 tablespoon dill, chopped

DIRECTIONS

1.   In your air fryer, combine the corn with the mango and the other ingredients, toss and cook at 390 degrees F for 12 minutes.

2.   Divide the mix into bowls and serve. NUTRITION: Calories 100, Fat 2, Fiber 5, Carbs 9,

Protein 6

Zucchini Caprese Rollups

Preparation time: 5 minutes Cooking time: 8 minutes

Servings: 8

INGREDIENTS

- 1 Zucchini, sliced thinly lengthwise

- 4 oz mozzarella cheese, sliced

- 1 tomato, sliced

- 2 Tbsp chopped fresh basil

- 2 Tbsp olive oil

DIRECTIONS

1.   Preheat your air fryer to 400 degrees F and prepare a

large baking dish with

foil.

2.   Lay the zucchini slices out on a clean work surface.

3.   Place a piece of tomato, cheese and a little basil on each

zucchini slice and then roll up to enclose the filling.

4.   Secure using a toothpick and then place the eggplant

rolls on the prepared foil lined baking dish.

5.   Drizzle with the olive oil and place in the air fryer to cook for 8 minutes. The zucchini should be lightly brown and the cheese melted. Serve warm.

NUTRITION: Calories 61, Total Fat 3g, Saturated Fat 1g, Total Carbs 5g, Net Carbs 4g, Protein 3g, Sugar 3g, Fiber 1g, Sodium 90mg, Potassium 178mg

Eggplant Parmesan Rollups

Preparation time: 5 minutes Cooking time: 8 minutes

Servings: 8

INGREDIENTS

- 1 eggplant, sliced thinly lengthwise

- 4 oz grated parmesan

- 1 tomato, sliced

- 2 Tbsp chopped fresh basil

- 2 Tbsp olive oil

DIRECTIONS

1.   Preheat your air fryer to 400 degrees F and prepare a large baking dish with foil.

2.   Lay the eggplant slices out on a clean work surface.

3.   Place a piece of tomato, cheese and a little basil on each eggplant slice and then roll up to enclose the filling.

4.   Secure using a toothpick and then place the eggplant rolls on the prepared foil lined baking dish.

5.   Drizzle with the olive oil and place in the air fryer to cook for 8 minutes. The eggplant should be lightly brown and the cheese melted. Serve warm.

NUTRITION: Calories 57, Total Fat 3g, Saturated Fat 1g, Total Carbs 4g, Net Carbs 3g, Protein 3g, Sugar 2g, Fiber 1g, Sodium 90mg, Potassium 178mg

Air Fryer Grilled Mexican Corn

Servings: 4

Cooking Time: 15 minutes

INGREDIENTS

- 4 pieces fresh corn on the cob

- ¼ teaspoon chili powder

- ½ teaspoon stone house seasoning

- ¼ cup chopped cilantro 1 lime cut into wedge

- ¼ cup cojita or feta cheese

DIRECTIONS

1. Preheat the air fryer at 3750F.

2. Place the grill pan accessory in the air fryer.

3. Season the corn with chili powder and stone house seasoning.

4. Place on the grill pan and cook for 15 minutes while flipping the corn halfway through the cooking time.

5. Serve the corn with cilantro, lime, and feta cheese.

NUTRITION: Calories:102; Carbs: 17g; Protein: 4g; Fat: 3g

Crispy and Spicy Grilled Broccoli in Air Fryer

Servings: 1

Cooking Time: 15 minutes

INGREDIENTS

- 1 head of broccoli, cut into florets

- 2 tablespoons yogurt

- 1 tablespoon chickpea flour

- Salt and pepper to taste

- ½ teaspoon red chili flakes

- 1tablespoon nutritional yeast

DIRECTIONS

1. Preheat the air fryer at 375oF.

2. Place the grill pan accessory in the air fryer.

3. Put all Ingredients in a Ziploc bag and shake until well combined.

4. Dump the ingredients on the grill pan and cook for 15 minutes until crispy.

NUTRITION: Calories: 96; Carbs: 16.9g; Protein: 7.1g; Fat: 1.3g

Grilled Zucchini with Mozzarella

Servings: 6

Cooking Time: 20 minutes

INGREDIENTS

•   3 medium zucchinis, sliced lengthwise 3 tablespoons extra virgin olive oil Salt and ground black pepper

•   18-ounce mozzarella ball, pulled into large pieces

•   2 tablespoons fresh dill

•   ¼ crushed red pepper

•   1 tablespoon lemon juice

DIRECTIONS

1   Preheat the air fryer at 3500F.

2   Place the grill pan accessory in the air fryer.

3   Drizzle the zucchini with olive oil and season with salt and pepper to taste.

4   Place on the grill pan and cook for 15 to 20 minutes.

5   Serve the zucchini with mozzarella, dill, red pepper and lemon juice.

NUTRITION: Calories:182; Carbs: 18.3g; Protein: 11.4g; Fat: 7.1g

Eggplant Tahini Rollups

Preparation time: 5 minutes Cooking time: 8 minutes

Servings: 8

INGREDIENTS

- 1 eggplant, sliced thinly lengthwise

- 4 oz mozzarella cheese, sliced

- ¼ cup tahini paste

- 2 Tbsp chopped fresh basil

- 2 Tbsp olive oil

DIRECTIONS

1. Preheat your air fryer to 400 degrees F and prepare a large baking dish with foil.

2. Lay the eggplant slices out on a clean work surface.

3. Spread tahini on each eggplant then top with a slice of cheese and a little basil on each eggplant slice and then roll up to enclose the filling.

4. Secure using a toothpick and then place the eggplant rolls on the prepared foil lined baking dish.

5.   Drizzle with the olive oil and place in the air fryer to cook for 8 minutes. The eggplant should be lightly brown and the cheese melted. Serve warm.

NUTRITION: Calories 68, Total Fat 4g, Saturated Fat 2g, Total Carbs 4g, Net Carbs 3g, Protein 4g, Sugar 2g, Fiber 1g, Sodium 105 Mg, Potassium 178mg

Grilled Tomato Melts

Servings: 3

Cooking Time: 20 minutes

INGREDIENTS

- 3 large tomatoes

- 4 ounces Monterey Jack cheese

- 1 yellow red bell pepper, chopped

- ¼ cup toasted almonds Salt and pepper to taste

DIRECTIONS

1   Preheat the air fryer at 3500F.

2   Place the grill pan accessory in the air fryer.

3   Slice the tops of the tomatoes and remove

4   the seeds to create hollow "cups."

5   In a mixing bowl, combine the cheese, bell pepper, and almonds.

6   Season with salt and pepper to taste.

7   Stuff the tomatoes with the cheese filling.

8   Place the stuffed tomatoes on the grill pan and cook for 15 to 20 minutes.

NUTRITION: Calories: 125; Carbs: 13g; Protein: 10g; Fat: 14g

Mushroom Lunch Lasagna

Preparation time: 5 minutes Cooking time: 15 minutes

Servings: 1

INGREDIENTS

- ½ large zucchini, sliced thinly

- ½ cup thinly sliced mushrooms

- 3 Tbsp keto marinara sauce

- 2 Tbsp ricotta, whole milk

- ¼ cup fresh chopped mozzarella

DIRECTIONS

1.   Preheat your air fryer to 400 degrees F.

2.   Get an oven safe large ramekin or mug.

3.   Lay some of the zucchini and mushroom slices in the bottom of the cup.

4.   Spread about 1 tablespoon of the ricotta on top of the zucchini then top with a tablespoon of the marinara sauce.

5.   Layer more zucchini and mushrooms on top of the marinara and repeat the layering process until you have used all the zucchini, mushrooms, ricotta and marinara.

6.   Top with the mozzarella.

7.   Place the lasagna in the oven and bake for 15 minutes or until the mozzarella is melted and bubbly. Enjoy hot

NUTRITION: Calories 343, Total Fat 24g, Saturated Fat 15g, Total Carbs 9g, Net Carbs 6g, Protein 20g, Sugar 4g, Fiber 2g, Sodium 562mg, Potassium 248g

Spicy Eggplant Rollups

Preparation time: 5 minutes Cooking time: 8 minutes

Servings: 8

INGREDIENTS

- 1 eggplant, sliced thinly lengthwise

- 4 oz parmesan cheese, sliced

- 1 tomato, sliced

- 2 Tbsp chopped fresh basil

- 2 Tbsp olive oil

- 1 tsp cayenne pepper

DIRECTIONS

1. Preheat your air fryer to 400 degrees F and prepare a large baking dish with foil.

2. Lay the eggplant slices out on a clean work surface.

3. Place a piece of tomato, cheese and a little basil on each eggplant slice and then roll up to enclose the filling.

4. Secure using a toothpick and then place the eggplant rolls on the prepared foil lined baking dish.

5.   Drizzle with the olive oil, sprinkle with the cayenne and place in the air fryer to cook for 8 minutes. The eggplant should be lightly brown and the cheese melted. Serve warm.

NUTRITION: Calories 60, Total Fat 3g, Saturated Fat 1g, Total Carbs 4g, Net Carbs 3g, Protein 3g, Sugar 2g, Fiber 1g, Sodium 90mg,

Potassium 178mg

Avocado Egg Salad

Preparation time: 5 minutes Cooking time: 16 minutes

Servings: 6

INGREDIENTS

- 6 Tbsp Mayonnaise

- 8 Large Eggs

- 2 Tbsp apple cider vinegar

- 1 tsp ground black pepper

- 1 tsp salt

- 1 avocado, chopped

DIRECTIONS

1. Preheat your air fryer to 250 degrees F.

2. Place a wire rack in the air fryer and place the eggs on top of the rack.

3. Cook for 16 minutes then remove the eggs and place them directly into an ice water bath to cool and stop the cooking process.

4. Peel the eggs and place in a large bowl.

5. Mash the eggs with a fork.

6. Add in the mayonnaise, cider vinegar, pepper and salt.

7.   Gently stir in the avocado and then serve chilled.

NUTRITION: Calories 289, Total Fat 22g, Saturated Fat 9g, Total Carbs 5g, Net Carbs 4g, Protein 12g, Sugar 0g, Fiber 1g, Sodium 488mg, Potassium 254g

Deviled Egg Salad

Preparation time: 5 minutes Cooking time: 16 minutes

Servings: 6

INGREDIENTS

• 6 Tbsp Mayonnaise

• 8 Large Eggs

• 2 Tbsp apple cider vinegar

• 1 tsp ground black pepper

• 1 tsp salt

• 1 tsp smoked paprika, ground

DIRECTIONS

1. Preheat your air fryer to 250 degrees F.

2. Place a wire rack in the air fryer and place the eggs on top of the rack.

3. Cook for 16 minutes then remove the eggs and place them directly into an ice water bath to cool and stop the cooking process.

4. Peel the eggs and place in a large bowl.

5. Mash the eggs with a fork.

6.   Add in the mayonnaise, cider vinegar, pepper, smoked paprika and salt

NUTRITION: Calories 189, Total Fat 12g, Saturated Fat 6g, Total Carbs 2g, Net Carbs 1g, Protein 12g, Sugar 0g, Fiber 1g, Sodium 489mg, Potassium 311g

Eggplant Caprese Rollups

Preparation time: 5 minutes Cooking time: 8 minutes

Servings: 8

INGREDIENTS

- 1 eggplant, sliced thinly lengthwise

- 4 oz mozzarella cheese, sliced

- 1 tomato, sliced

- 2 Tbsp chopped fresh basil

- 2 Tbsp olive oil

DIRECTIONS

1. Preheat your air fryer to 400 degrees F and prepare a large baking dish with foil.

2. Lay the eggplant slices out on a clean work surface.

3. Place a piece of tomato, cheese and a little basil on each eggplant slice and then roll up to enclose the filling.

4. Secure using a toothpick and then place the eggplant rolls on the prepared foil lined baking dish.

5. Drizzle with the olive oil and place in the air fryer to cook for 8 minutes. The eggplant should be lightly brown and the cheese melted. Serve warm.

NUTRITION: Calories 59, Total Fat 3g, Saturated Fat 1g, Total Carbs 4g, Net Carbs 3g, Protein 3g, Sugar 2g, Fiber 1g, Sodium 90mg, Potassium 178mg

Grilled Cauliflower Bites

Servings: 1

Cooking Time: 15 minutes

INGREDIENTS

- ½ cups cauliflower florets

- 1 tablespoon olive oil

- 2tablespoons nutritional yeast Salt and pepper to taste

DIRECTIONS

1. Preheat the air fryer at 3750F.

2. Place the grill pan accessory in the air fryer.

3. In a mixing bowl, toss all ingredients until well-combined.

4. Dump the vegetables on to the grill pan and cook for 10 to 15 minutes.

NUTRITION: Calories: 81; Carbs: 6.5g; Protein: 4.2g; Fat: 4.9g

Avocado Salad

Preparation time: 5 minutes Cooking time: 5 minutes

Servings: 4

INGREDIENTS

- red onion, sliced

- cups avocado, peeled, pitted and cubed 1 cup cherry tomatoes, halved

- 2 tablespoons avocado oil Juice of 1 lime

- Salt and black pepper to the taste 1 cup walnuts, chopped

- 1 tablespoon chives, chopped

DIRECTIONS

In your air fryer, mix the avocado with the tomatoes and the other ingredients, toss, cook at 400 degrees F for 5 minutes, divide into bowls and serve.

NUTRITION: Calories 151, Fat 4, Fiber 6,

Carbs 9,

Protein 4

Spicy Sriracha Egg Salad

Preparation time: 5 minutes Cooking time: 16 minutes

Servings: 6

INGREDIENTS

- 6 Tbsp Mayonnaise

- 8 Large Eggs

- 2 Tbsp apple cider vinegar

- 1 tsp ground black pepper

- 1 tsp salt

- 1 Tbsp sriracha sauce

DIRECTIONS

- Preheat your air fryer to 250 degrees F.

- Place a wire rack in the air fryer and place the eggs on top of the rack.

- Cook for 16 minutes then remove the eggs and place them directly into an ice water bath to cool and stop the cooking process.

- Peel the eggs and place in a large bowl.

- Mash the eggs with a fork.

- Add in the mayonnaise, cider vinegar, pepper, sriracha and salt

NUTRITION: Calories 189, Total Fat 12g, Saturated Fat 6g, Total Carbs 2g, Net Carbs 1g, Protein 12g, Sugar 1g, Fiber 1g, Sodium 467mg, Potassium 289g

Cheesy Brussels Sprout Salad

Preparation time: 7 minutes Cooking time: 15 minutes

Servings: 4

INGREDIENTS

- 1 pound Brussel sprouts, sliced in quarters

- 1 tsp minced, fresh rosemary

- ¼ cup olive oil

- 1 Tbsp apple cider vinegar

- 2 Tbsp lemon juice

- ½ tsp Dijon mustard

- ½ tsp kosher salt

- ½ cup grated parmesan cheese

DIRECTIONS

1.   Preheat your air fryer to 450 degrees F and line the air fryer tray or baking pan with foil.

2.   Toss the Brussels sprouts with the rosemary and olive oil and place on the prepared tray.

3.   Roast in the air fryer for 15 minutes.

4.   Place the hot, roasted sprouts in a large bowl and add the remaining ingredients to make a dressing. Toss well and serve hot or cold.

NUTRITION: Calories 209, Total Fat 23g, Saturated Fat 6g, Total Carbs 14g, Net Carbs 7g, Protein 36g, Sugar 3g, Fiber 7g, Sodium 324mg, Potassium 578g

Eggplant Zucchini Rollups

Preparation time: 5 minutes Cooking time: 8 minutes

Servings: 8

INGREDIENTS

- 1 eggplant, sliced thinly lengthwise

- 4 oz mozzarella cheese, sliced

- 1 zucchini, sliced lengthwise

- 2 Tbsp chopped fresh basil

- 2 Tbsp olive oil

DIRECTIONS

1.   Preheat your air fryer to 400 degrees F and prepare a large baking dish with foil.

2.   Lay the eggplant slices out on a clean work surface.

3.   Place a piece of zucchini, cheese and a little basil on each eggplant slice and then roll up to enclose the filling.

4.   Secure using a toothpick and then place the eggplant rolls on the prepared foil lined baking dish.

5.   Drizzle with the olive oil and place in the air fryer to cook for 8 minutes. The eggplant should be lightly brown and the cheese melted. Serve warm.

NUTRITION: Calories 68, Total Fat 3g, Saturated Fat 1g, Total Carbs 5g, Net Carbs 4g, Protein 3g, Sugar 1g, Fiber 1g, Sodium 90mg, Potassium 178mg

Chips

Preparation time: 10-20 minutes Cooking time: 30-45 minutes

Servings: 8

INGREDIENTS

- 1500g of fresh potatoes

- Fine salt to taste

- 1 tsp peanut oil

DIRECTIONS

1. Peel the potatoes and cut them into sticks of approximately 1 cm per side.

2. Put the cut potatoes in water for a few minutes and rinse thoroughly.

3. Drain and clean well with a paper towel.

4. Pour the potatoes and the correct amount of oil in the pan.

5. Cook for 37/40 minutes at 180oC. Salt then serve.

NUTRITION: Calories 365 Fat 17g Carbohydrates 48g Sugars 0.3g Protein 4g Cholesterol 0mg

French Fries with Paprika

Preparation time: 10-20 minutes Cooking time: 15-30 minutes

Servings: 8

INGREDIENTS

• 700g of carrots

• 1 tsp sweet paprika

• 1 tsp oil

DIRECTIONS

1. Peel the carrots and cut them into sticks.

2. Add carrots and paprika in the basket. Set the temperature to 1800C.

3. Cook the carrots for about 20 minutes (time may vary depending on the size of the carrots).

NUTRITION: Calories 299 Carbohydrates 33g Sugars 3g Fat 16g Protein 7g Cholesterol 163 Mg

635. Frozen French Fries

Cooking time: 15-30 minutes Servings: 8

INGREDIENTS

• 1000g Standard French fries (10 X 10) mm frozen

• Fine salt to taste

DIRECTIONS:

1.   Preheat the air fryer at 1500C.

2.   Let cook for 27 minutes: salt and serve.

NUTRITION: Calories 150.0 Fat 0.0 G Carbohydrate 20.0 G

Sugars0.0 G Protein2.0 G Cholesterol 0.0 Mg

Potato Salad

Preparation time: 4 minutes Cooking time: 25 minutes

Servings: 4

INGREDIENTS

- 1 pound sweet potatoes, peeled and cut into wedges

- 1 cup baby spinach

- 1 cup cherry tomatoes, halved

- 1 cup black olives, pitted and halved 1 tablespoon olive oil

- 1 teaspoon hot paprika 1 tablespoon lime juice

- Salt and black pepper to the taste

DIRECTIONS

1. In your air fryer, combine the potatoes with the spinach and the other ingredients, toss and cook at 400 degrees F for 25 minutes.

2. Divide into bowls and serve hot. NUTRITION: Calories 151, Fat 4, Fiber 7, Carbs 12, Protein 6

Beans in sauce

Preparation time: 0-10 minutes Cooking time: 15-30 minutes

Servings: 8

INGREDIENTS

- 500g canned beans

- 300g of tomato puree

- ½ carrot

- 1 onion

- ½ sprig of rosemary

- Salt and pepper to taste

- 1 tsp olive oil

DIRECTIONS

1. Prepare a chopped carrot and onion and place it inside the cooking tray with rosemary. Grease the basket with the oil.

2. Set the air fryer to 150oC and brown for 4 min.

3. Add the drained beans from your vegetable water and rinse thoroughly, simmer for another 3 min.

4. Add the tomato, ½ glass of water, salt and pepper and continue cooking for another 13 minutes.

NUTRITION: Calories 270 Fat 1g Carbohydrates 53g Sugars 14g Protein 14g Cholesterol 0mg

Spicy Potatoes

Preparation time: 10-20 minutes Cooking time: 30-45 minutes

Servings: 8

INGREDIENTS

- 1250g of fresh potatoes

- 10g sweet paprika

- Tomato puree

- 2 tbsp vinegar

- Salt and pepper to taste

DIRECTIONS

1.   Peel the potatoes and cut them into 1 cm cubes on each side. Put the potatoes in the water for a few minutes and rinse them well. Drain and clean with a paper towel.

2.   Pour the potatoes, rosemary, and the exact amount of oil inside the tank, salt, and pepper.

3.   Set the air fryer to 1600C and cook for 25 min.

4.   Add the paprika, tomato puree and vinegar, then finish cooking and simmer for another 10 minutes.

5.   Prepare the "tapas" by piercing the potatoes with toothpicks.

NUTRITION: Calories 250 Carbohydrates 33g Fat 11g Sugars

0g Protein 4g Cholesterol 0mg

Tomato and Shrimp Salad

Preparation time: 6 minutes Cooking time: 6

minutes Servings: 4

INGREDIENTS

- 1 pound cherry tomatoes, halved

- ½ pound shrimp, peeled and deveined Juice of 1 lime

- 1 cup baby kale

- 2 green onions, chopped 2 tomatoes, cubed

- jalapeno pepper, chopped 1 tablespoon olive oil

- teaspoons chili powder

- Salt and black pepper to the taste

DIRECTIONS

1. In a pan that fits your air fryer, mix the tomatoes with the shrimp, oil and the other ingredients, toss, introduce the pan in the fryer and cook at 400 degrees F for 6 minutes.

2. Divide the mix into bowls and serve. NUTRITION: Calories 200, Fat 4, Fiber 7, Carbs

12, Protein 6

Bell Peppers Salad

Preparation time: 10 minutes Cooking time: 15 minutes

Servings: 4

INGREDIENTS

- 2 red bell peppers, cut into strips

- 2 green bell peppers, cut into strips 2 orange bell

peppers, cut into strips 1 cup cherry tomatoes, halved

- cup baby spinach Juice of 1 lime

- tablespoons olive oil

- Salt and black pepper to the taste

DIRECTIONS

1. In a pan that fits your air fryer, mix the peppers with

the tomatoes and the other ingredients, toss, introduce the

pan in the fryer and cook at 360 degrees F for 15 minutes.

2. Divide into bowls and serve. NUTRITION: Calories 161,

Fat 7, Fiber 6, Carbs

12, Protein 7

Garlic Carrots and Spinach Salad

Preparation time: 10 minutes Cooking time: 15 minutes

Servings: 4

INGREDIENTS

•   1 pound baby carrots, peeled and sliced 1 cup baby

spinach

•   1 cup corn

•   Juice of ½ lemon

•   1 tablespoon olive oil 6 garlic cloves, minced

•   1 tablespoon balsamic vinegar Salt and black pepper to

the taste

DIRECTIONS

1.   In the air fryer's pan, mix the carrots with the spinach

and the other ingredients, toss and cook at 380 degrees F for

15 minutes.

2.   Divide into bowls and serve.

Sprouts and Pomegranate Mix

Preparation time: 5 minutes Cooking time: 10 minutes

Servings: 4

INGREDIENTS

*   1 pound Brussels sprouts, trimmed and halved

*   1 cup pomegranate seeds 1 cup baby spinach

*   tablespoon avocado oil

*   tablespoons balsamic vinegar 1 teaspoon chili powder

*   Salt and black pepper to the taste

DIRECTIONS

1.   In the air fryer's pan, mix the sprouts with the pomegranate seeds and the other ingredients, toss and cook at 380 degrees F for 10 minutes.

2.   Divide into bowls and serve. NUTRITION: Calories 141, Fat 3, Fiber 4, Carbs

11, Protein 4

Potatoes, Beets and Carrots

Preparation time: 10-20 minutes Cooking time:

30-45 minutes

Servings: 6

INGREDIENTS

- 300g beet

- 300 g of carrots

- 300 g of potatoes

- 2 cloves of garlic

- Rosemary to taste

- Salt to taste

- Pepper to taste

DIRECTIONS

Clean, wash all vegetables (beets, carrots, and potatoes) and

cut them into pieces of 2 to 3 cm. Put the garlic clove, chopped

vegetables, rosemary and spray the basket; Season with salt

and pepper.

Cook for about 35 minutes at 1500C. NUTRITION: Calories

170.5 Fat 7.1 G Carbohydrate 26.5 G Sugars 9.5 G Protein3.4 G

Cholesterol 0.0 Mg

Cauliflower and Pomegranate Mix

Preparation time: 6 minutes Cooking time: 12 minutes

Servings: 4

- 1 pound cauliflower florets 1 cup pomegranate seeds 1 tablespoon lime juice
- 1 tablespoon orange juice 1 tablespoon olive oil
- Salt and black pepper to the taste 2 tablespoons chives, chopped

DIRECTIONS

1. In your air fryer's pan, mix the cauliflower with the pomegranate seeds and the other ingredients, toss, and cook at 400 degrees F for 12 minutes.

2. Divide into bowls and serve. NUTRITION: Calories 200, Fat 7, Fiber 5, Carbs 17, Protein 7

CPSIA information can be obtained
at www.ICGtesting.com
Printed in the USA
LVHW011203090621
689681LV00003B/258